The Art of
Painting

Temima Gezari
Drawing and Sculpture

Edited by Daniel Gezari

The Art of Temima Gezari
Painting, Drawing and Sculpture

Daniel Gezari, Editor

Library of Congress Cataloging-in-Publication Data
Gezari, Temima, 1905-
     The art of Temima Gezari.

     Includes index.
     1. Gezari, Temima, 1905-   .   I. Gezari, Daniel Y.
II. Title.
N6537.G44A4   1985   709'.2'4   85-31536
ISBN 0-9616269-0-9

Graphic Design and Color Photography by
Daniel Gezari

Printed by

Searles Graphics, Inc.
East Patchogue, NY 11772

Published by

Studio Workshop Press
66 Noah's Path
Rocky Point, NY 11778

Made in U.S.A.
First Edition 1985

Table of Contents

Editor's Note i
Biographic Sketch iii
Index of Works vi

Part I (1925-1939):
Figure drawings 1
Taos drawings and gouaches 7
Jerusalem 1934, 1938 12
Lithographs - Lower East Side 20
Gloucester gouaches 28
Murals 36

Part II (1939-1953):
Sculpture 42
Oil paintings 52
Bronze sculpture 59

Part III (1953-1970):
Beachstone Series 65
Terra cotta and bronze sculpture 73

Part IV (1970-1985):
Totem Series 97
Behold the People 104
Africa Series 110
Small bronzes 112
Nature Series 115
Family Series 121
Mask Series 125
China Series 128
Abstractions 135
Childhood Fantasy Series 137
Israel Series 138
Animal Series 139
Woman Series 140

Catalogue of Works 142

I am grateful to the following people for their contribution to this project —

Faye Lourenso for her skill in the production of the book, Gary Lorandini for his fine camera work, Reba Siegel for effective production management, Ken Searles for his high printing standards, Phyllis Bayne for editorial assistance, Zvi Gezari for his dedicated photographic work, and to Walter Gezari for his advice and support.

Special thanks to Geyza Sarkany, who photographed several of the sculpture series, including the Africa Series, the Totems, and the Nature Series.

Editor's Note

For several years I have wanted to do a retrospective book of Temima Gezari's work. This collection, spanning her career from 1925 to the present, gives an insight into the evolution and context of her ideas. The book is arranged chronologically. Her philosophical position begins with her interest in the human being as an individual, moves to human social interactions, and emerges as a statement on the elegance of nature.

It is significant that she spent much of her life as a working professional and an artist in a period when these areas were generally closed to women.

The majority of the photographs in this volume were taken over the years by my father, Zvi. Only a fraction of Temima's artwork appears here. However, each major series of painting, drawings, and sculptures she has done is represented by at least one significant piece. We no longer have many of her works, therefore sizes had to be estimated for some of the pieces.

The names of places cited in the figure captions indicate where each piece was done; those not attributed were made in her studio in Rocky Point beginning in 1947. She fires her clay sculpture in a special kiln Zvi built. He made the first casting of *Leaping Lena*. The rest of the bronzes have been cast at the Modern Art Foundry in New York City.

Temima is a humanist. She has discovered, and actively promotes, an important approach to the development of children's full human potential—to recognize their great innate creativity, and encourage them to express it. She has dedicated her life to helping others find this creative self, while exploring the dimensions of her own spirit.

The biographical sketch that follows only touches upon a few significant events of her life. Today, at the age of 80, she continues to work as artist and educator with skill and energy. She has brought us an opportunity to recognize in her art, and in ourselves, the creative capacity of the human being.

Daniel Gezari
December 21, 1985

*Temima Gezari's sketches of her
neighborhood in Brownsville, age 15.*

Biographical Sketch

Temima Gezari came to the United States as a nine month old baby. She was born Fruma Nimtzowitz on December 21, 1905 in Pinsk, Russia. She grew up in Brownsville, Brooklyn with her parents, sister Etta and brother Ruby. The family lived in the back room of her father's hardware store on Pitkin Avenue. When things got better they moved to an apartment above the store, which was heated by a coal stove in the kitchen.

Her mother Bella (nee Cohen) was a gentle, traditional and observant woman who loved things of beauty. She appreciated Temima's art but gave the practical problems of life higher priority, and never understood the importance of it until she saw Temima's synagogue mural in 1935.

Her father Yisroel was a serious and philosophical man who became progressively more disillusioned over the condition of the world. He worked hard, and often found comfort with his friends at the Labor Lyceum. He was not a religious man, yet he placed great importance on culture and tradition.

Her father recognized her artistic talent as a very young child and actively encouraged it. At the age of seven he took her into Manhattan to the Educational Alliance with the hope of enrolling her in art classes. He told her he would take her to school every day from Brooklyn by train, a personal gesture which had a powerful effect on little Temima, her first realization that her art was being taken seriously. As it turned out there were no art classes for children, so her father invested in art supplies and piano lessons for her instead.

She tells of an experience at about that time which was later to play an important part in shaping her approach toward people, education and art.

"The day that my third-grade teacher in public school came into the room with an open book in her hand, went to the blackboard and copied from it the picture of a bird, was a very crucial day in my life. The bird was sitting on the branch of a tree. It was lamely drawn, a bad copy from the sample in the book. The teacher handed out sheets of drawing paper and crayons and told us to draw the bird. 'The one who does it best,' she said, 'will get a gold star.'

"We all went to work. I looked at the bird on the blackboard. It seemed to me so clumsy, so lacking in grace, it could never spread its wings and fly. I was a very young child but I knew that the strange creature on the blackboard was not right, and my instinct refused to make me a partner in that miserable process. So I did not copy the bird on the blackboard, but drew my own. Needless to say, I did not get the gold star...but my bird was flying!"

M'raglim, small tapestry, age 14.

Temima Gezari graduated from Brooklyn Girls High School in 1921, the Teacher's Institute of the Jewish Theological Seminary of America in 1925, and the Master Institute of United Arts in 1930. She also studied at Columbia University, the New School for Social Research, and Hunter College.

Her first art teacher was Bulah Stevenson, an inspiring woman who had a great influence on Temima's early development as an artist. She went on to study art at the Parsons New York School of Fine and Applied Arts with Emil Bisttram and Howard Giles (1923 - 1927), the Educational Alliance in New York with Raphael Soyer (1926), and the Art Students League in New York.

In the Summer of 1931 Temima bought a Model A Ford roadster she named "Pegasus" and drove with two girlfriends to Taos, New Mexico, to study with her teacher Emil Bisttram at the Toas School of Art. The drive was an unheard of venture for single women, and exceptional in most other respects since at that time there were no highways across the country.

In the early thirties she studied art and traveled extensively in the United States, Mexico and Europe, as well as Jordan, Syria, Egypt, Lebanon and Palestine.

In 1933, when Temima was a student at the Master Institute of United Arts, the Mexican muralist Diego Rivera was painting in one of the new Rockefeller Center buildings in New York City. Temima went with a group of her classmates to observe the famous painter at work, only to learn that Rivera was painting only at night when the building was closed. Temima argued with the guard, why hadn't they been told this when they made arrangements for the class visit? Another voice interrupted, "Give this girl a pass to enter the building anytime." It was Diego Rivera. "What about my friends?" asked Temima. "Let them be as angry as you are," said Rivera, "and they will get passes too." Temima went on to spend many inspiring weeks on the scaffold with Rivera.

He invited her to paint with him that fall on the mural for the last wall of the National Palace in Mexico City. She packed and drove to Taos again, enroute to Mexico, only to learn that the project had been postponed. Rather than return to New York, Temima went instead to paint for the year of 1934 in Jerusalem.

A person who exerted a great influence on her professional life was Professor Mordecai Kaplan. In 1935, as Dean of the Teachers Institute of the Jewish Theological Seminary, he appointed her to the faculty, where she taught art education and art history for forty-two years.

In 1935, Dr. Kaplan gave Temima a wall in the Synagogue of the Society for the Advancement of Judiasm on which to paint a mural, a very exciting move at the time. It was the beginning of a new era of synagogue decoration. There had been a traditional ban on representational decoration in synagogues, based on a literal interpretation of the Second Commandment. The mural stirred tremendous controversy. Dr. Kaplan, one of the greatest theologians of the twentieth century, took a great deal of criticism for the project but successfully defended the position that art had a rightful place in the spiritual life of the Jewish community.

Temima met Zvi on the Kibbutz Mishmar Haemek transport bus when she arrived to paint as artist-in-residence in 1936. The bus was full, so the driver invited her to sit on a can next to him. She thought this would be great fun, to be able to talk to the driver and see the sights. Just as she sat down, a very handsome young man called from the back to offer her his seat. She declined, but he persisted. So Zvi rode on the gas can, chatting with the driver, while Temima simmered with anger in his seat. She swore she would never have anything to do with that fresh guy again. They were married in Tel Aviv in 1938 and moved back to New York, where their sons Daniel and Walter were born in 1942 and 1944.

Zvi was born in Poland in 1910 and went to Palestine in 1928 where he worked building new kibbutzim and studied. In 1938 he arrived in New York speaking only a few words of English. On his first day in New York he registered for engineering courses at Columbia University. By 1940 he spoke standard American English without any trace of an accent. He became an industrial engineer, and went on to develop and manage a large steel fabrication factory. Zvi is a very progressive man, deeply interested in history and science. In 1954 he built a telescope for Albert Einstein.

In 1940, Dr. Alexander Dushkin asked Temima to join the newly formed Jewish Education Committee, now the Board of Jewish Education, as the Director of the Department of Art Education. It was an important step in the development of art as a tool for teaching Jewish tradition, and for helping all children develop themselves as creative human beings.

In the Spring of 1947, Temima and Zvi took the boys for a ride on Long Island, to the beach town of Rocky Point. With the last ten dollars in his pocket, Zvi gave a deposit to a farmer for a piece of apple orchard on a hill overlooking the Sound. The house, studio and observatory he designed and built there, have been the creative and idealistic focal point of the family and local community ever since.

Temima Gezari has had one-woman shows in New York, Washington, Philadelphia, Cleveland and Jerusalem. She established the Junior Gallery at the Jewish Museum in New York (1950-1963) and has created exhibitions of children's art every year since 1940, giving children an opportunity to show their work for the sake of their individual growth and happiness, and to provide them an opportunity for wholesome and creative community participation.

Her book, *Footprints and New Worlds* (1957), now in its fourth edition, deals with her philosophy of education and child development through her experiences in art with children and adults.

Temima Gezari - 1934

Index of Works:

Abstraction 116
Abstraction #1 135
Abstraction #2 135
Africa Series 110
African Girl 44
African Plant 116
After the Raid 131
"Am Matza et ha Moledet, Shav Adam L'Adama" (plaque) 43
American Indian Totem 98
Anatomy Series 115
Angel, Flying 81
Angel, Little 90
Animal Series 139
Arab Mother 131
At the Beach (Behold the People Series) 105, 107
At the Wailing Wall 76
At the Well 77
American Eagle - Crucifixion 132
Bag Lady 140
Barley 116
Bathing Beauty 66
Beach Stone Series 65
Behold the People Series 104
Berry Vine 116
Biblical Women Series 140
Big Business - Cigarette Vendor 16
Big Business - Sabal (Porter) 16
Big Business - Shoe Repair Man 16
Birches 116
Birth 94
Boy with accordian 131
Boy with Hoe 131
Breeder 140
Bukharian Man 131
Bukarian Woman 131
Cain and Abel 51

Capillaries 116
Carousel 90
Cat 66
Cell 116
Childhood Fantasy Series 138
China Series 128
Circle and the Egg Series 115
Circle in a Square 6
Column of Peace 100
Concave and Convex 94
Conservation Totem 98
Conversation 88
Convolutions 116
Daniel - Age 7 52
Dancers (Behold the People Series) 107
Dancing Hassidim 91
Deborah the Judge 140
Derelicts (Behold the People Series) 106
Disc - What's the Good Word? 100
Donkey Ballet 13
Donkeys 14
Dormant 34
Driftwood Bird 72
Egyptian Mother 12
Elmolo Mother and Child 111
Elmolo Youth 111
Family (Behold the People Series) 106
Family Circle 50
Father and First Born 48
Fern 117
Figure 1
Figure - Diagonals 1
Fishermen 29
Flag Totem 101
Flying Angel 81
Foetus 94
Four Eves 51
Four Sisters 11

Four Sketches - Lower East Side 20
Freedom Song 75
Fruits of War 86
Generations Totem 98
Glouscester Waterfront 28
Goat 93
Going to School - China 133
Golden Calf 95
Gossip 87
Grapes of Wrath 55
Grandfather's Blessing 131
Ground Cover 116
Ha Magish 12
Had Gadya 93
Harvest Mural 37
Harvest Dance 130
Hassidic Couple 131
Hassidic Ecstacy 92
Hassidic Newlyweds 19
Head 1
Head - Diagonals 1
High Holiday Totem 98
House of My Teacher Emil Bisstram 7
Hunger Totem 98
"Im Lo Achshav, Eimatai?" (plaque) 43
In the Street (Behold the People Series) 106
Indian Women 9
Indian Woman in Doorway 27
Israel Series 130
Janet and Vanessa 122
Jericho 12
Job 89
Judiac Totem 99
Judiaca (Behold the People Series) 108
Juggler 69
Jungle Roots 114
Kibbutz Father 131
Kibbutz Mother 131

King Saul   91
Kiss   85
Lament   127
Landscape in Triangles   10
Land of Israel Mural   38
Land of Israel Mural (pencil study)   40
Leaping Lena   47
Little Angel   90
Little David   137
Little Presser   23
Love Not War Totem   101
Love Not War Totem - Fish for Shabbat   21
Lower East Side - Four Sketches   20
Lower East Side - The World Situation   21
Lower East Side - Under the Bridge   22
Male and Female   83
Masai Warrior   111
Mask Series   125
Maze   116
Mediation   73
Miriam   44
Moment of Silence   71
Morning Song   59
Moses   80
Mother and Baby   129
Mother and Child   102
Mother and Second Born   48
Mural, *Harvest*   37
Mural, *Land of Israel*   37
Mural, *Traveling to Rocky Point*   53
Mussel Shell   117
My Grandfather (drawing)   3
My Mother   62
My Studio   7
National Organization of Women   140
Nature Series   115
New Atlas   136
Newsboy   45
Night Prowler   60
Night Riders   66

Old City of Jerusalem   12
On the Bus (Behold the People Series)   106
On the Dock   30
Panther   79
Pay Day   33
Peace Totem   98
Performers (Behold the People Series)   107
Pillar of Salt   91
Pirjo and Suvi   122
Primitive Family   87
Prometheus Bound   90
Purim Shpreter   130
Rachel   140
Rebbi and Rebitzen   92
Rebecca   140
Reclining Figure   5
Refugees   87
Rocks - Monhegan Island   6
Rosie the Lobsterman   31
Ruth and Naomi   140
Sabal   131
Sage   17
Sails   90
Sarah   140
Satat   15
Seated Nude   4
Seisal   116
Sex Symbol   140
Shabbat Totem   98
Shabbos Shpatziv   25
Shalom (bowl)   43
Six Sketches at the Beach   35
Small Bronzes   113
Spanish Dancer   68
Sports (Behold the People Series)   107
Stabile   119
Stampede   67
Standing Figure   5
Standing Nude   4

Stirring   34
Stone Cutter   49
Struggle   34
Study of a Head   5
Suffragettes   140
Sugar Cane   116
Suvi (Family Series)   121
Suvi in Daniel's Hand   122
Synagogue Mural - *Land of Israel*   38
Students Applaud Visitors   128
Sister and Brother   129
Taos Pueblo #2   8
Tax Totem   101
Three Generations   19
Time to Dance   57
Time to Embrace   57
Torso (drawing)   4
Torso (terra cotta)   82
Totem Series   97
Traveling to Rocky Point (mural)   53
Tree of Life (Circle on a Square)   6
Tree Study   6
Under the Bridge (Lower East Side)   22
Union Label   140
Vertical and Horizontal #2   10
Vanessa (Family Series)   121
Vanessa - After the Bath   123
Vanessa - Newborn   123
Walter - Age 5   42
Wash Day - Kibbutz   26
Winged Victory   103
Woman of Valor   140
Woman Series   140
Woman's Head   42
Worker   128
World Situation (Lower East Side)   21
Yeminite Bride   131
Yeshiva Bachurim   91
Yizkor   87

Seated Nude, 1925 (New York),
pencil drawing, 18″ × 12″.

Standing Nude, *1927 (New York),*
chalk drawing, 18″ × 12″.

Torso, *1927 (New York), chalk*
drawing, 18″ × 12″.

My Grandfather, 1932 (New York), pencil drawing, 15" × 12".

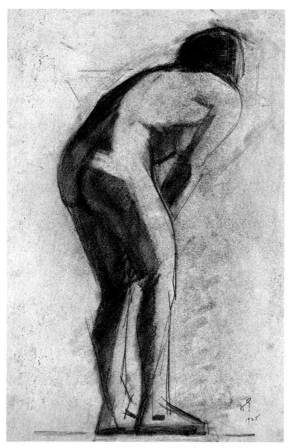

Figure, 1925 (New York), pencil
drawing, 18″ × 12″.

Figure - Diagonals, 1926 (New York),
pencil drawing, 18″ × 12″.

Head, 1927 (New York), chalk
drawing, 18″ × 12″.

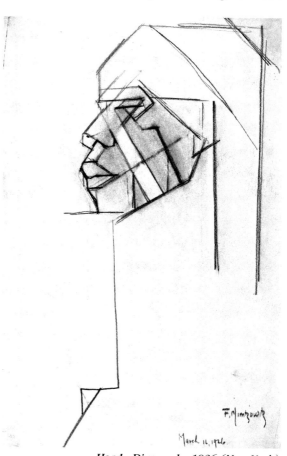

Head - Diagonals, 1926 (New York),
pencil drawing, 18″ × 12″.

Study of a Head, 1927 (New York),
pencil drawing, 15″ × 13″.

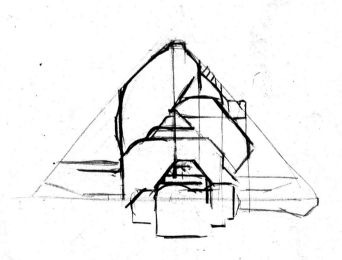

Reclining Figure, 1927 (New York),
pencil drawing, 18″ × 12″.

Standing Figure, 1927 (New York),
pencil drawing, 18″ × 12″.

Rocks - Monhegan Island, 1930 (Maine),
pencil drawing, 15" × 13".

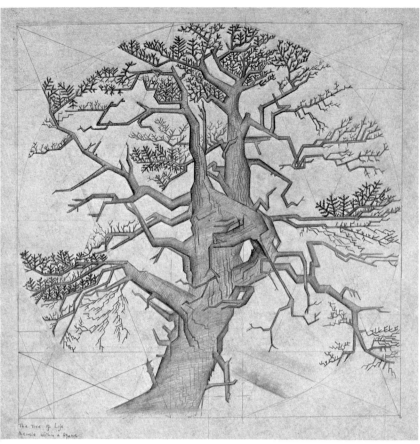

Tree of Life (Circle in a Square), 1930
(Maine), pencil drawing, 15" × 13".

Tree Study, 1932 (Taos), pencil
drawing, 21" × 15".

The House of My Teacher Emil Bisttram, *1931*
(Taos), pencil drawing, 9″ × 11½″.

My Studio, *1931 (Taos), pencil drawing, 9″ × 11½″.*

Taos Pueblo #2, 1931 (Taos), pencil drawing, 11″ × 15″.

Indian Women, 1932 (Taos), pencil drawing, 13″ × 11″.

Landscape in Triangles, *1932 (New York),*
pencil drawing, 10" × 14".

Vertical and Horizontal #2, *1932 (New York),*
pencil drawing, 10" × 10".

Four Sisters*, 1932 (Taos), lithographic pencil drawing, 19" × 12".*

Egyptian Mother, 1934 (Jerusalem),
pencil drawing, 24″ × 18″.
Collection Mae and Mac Liss

Jericho, 1934 (Jerusalem), pencil
drawing, 18″ × 12″.

The Old City of Jerusalem, 1934 (Jerusalem),
pencil drawing, 20″ × 14″.

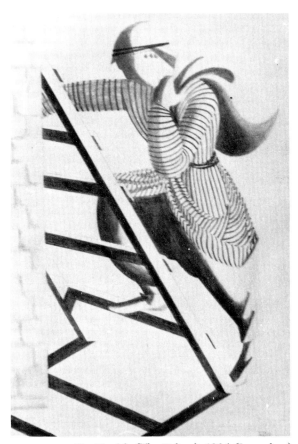

Ha Magish (The Helper), 1934 (Jerusalem),
pencil drawing, 24″ × 18″.

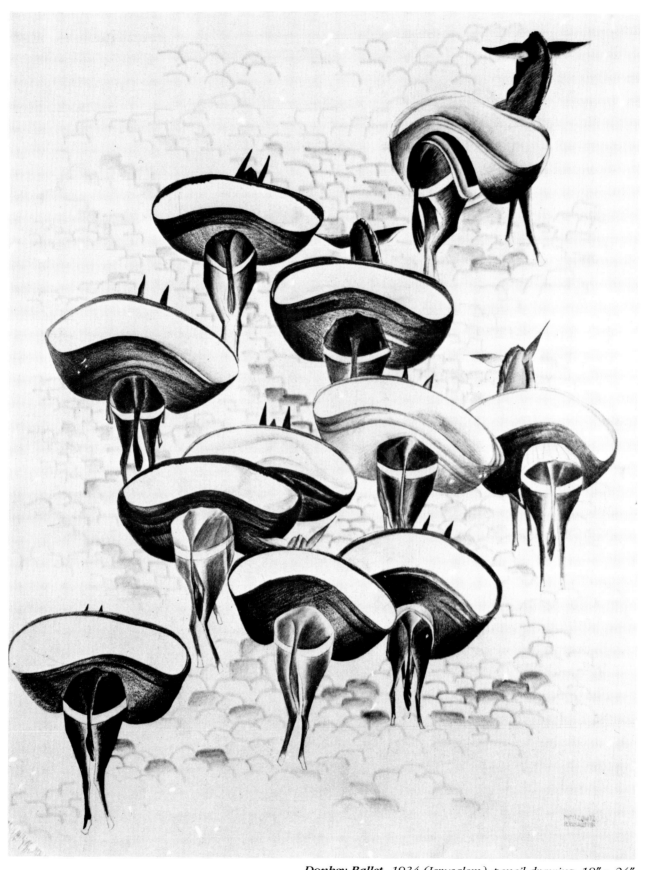

Donkey Ballet, *1934 (Jerusalem), pencil drawing, 18″ × 24″.*
Collection of Dr. and Mrs. Ira Yanowitz

Donkeys, *1934, Jerusalem, pencil drawing, 18" × 24".*
Collection of Daniel Gezari

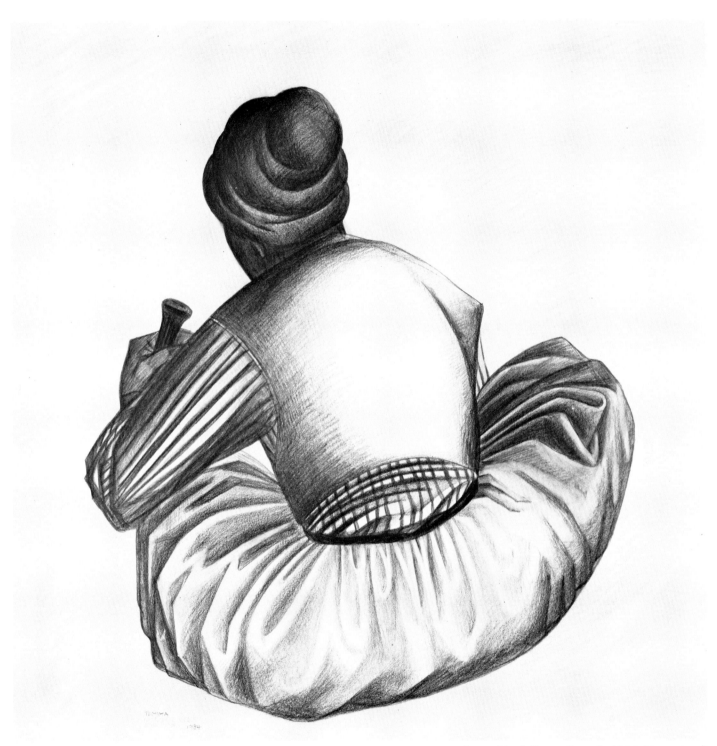

Satat (Arab Stone Cutter), 1934 (Jerusalem),
pencil drawing, 20″ × 20″.

Big Business - Cigarette Vendor, *1938,*
(Tel Aviv), pencil drawing, 17″ × 23″.

Big Business - Shoe Repair Man, *1938,*
(Tel Aviv), pencil drawing, 17″ × 23″.

Big Business - Sabal (Porter), *1938,*
(Tel Aviv), pencil drawing, 17″ × 24″.

The Sage, *1934 (Jerusalem), pencil drawing, 18″ × 12″.*

Hassidic Newlyweds, 1934 *(Jerusalem)*,
pencil drawing, 30″ × 24″.

***Three Generations**, 1934 (Jerusalem), pencil drawing, 30" × 24".*
Collection of Daniel Gezari

Four Sketches - Lower East Side, 1931 (New York), pen and
ink studies for lithographs, each 8½″ × 12½″.

Fish for Shabbat (Lower East Side), *1935*
(New York), lithograph, 15″ × 10″.

The World Situation (Lower East Side), *1935*
(New York), lithograph, 19″ × 15″.

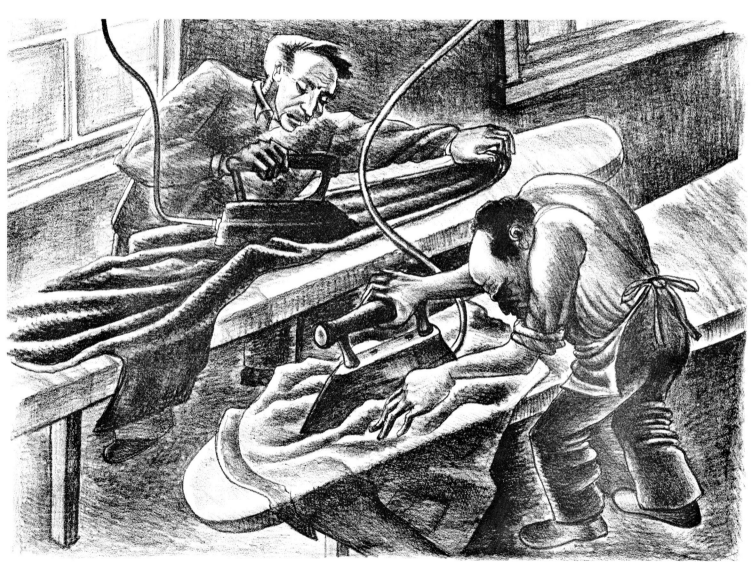

The Little Presser, 1935 (New York), lithograph, 18″ × 13″.

"Sabbath Promenade" Jerusalem

Tamima Gezari

Shabbos Shpatzir *(Sabbath Promenade), 1934 (Jerusalem),*
lithograph based on 1934 pencil drawing, 19" × 13".

Wash Day - Kibbutz, 1938 (New York), lithograph, 15″ × 11″.

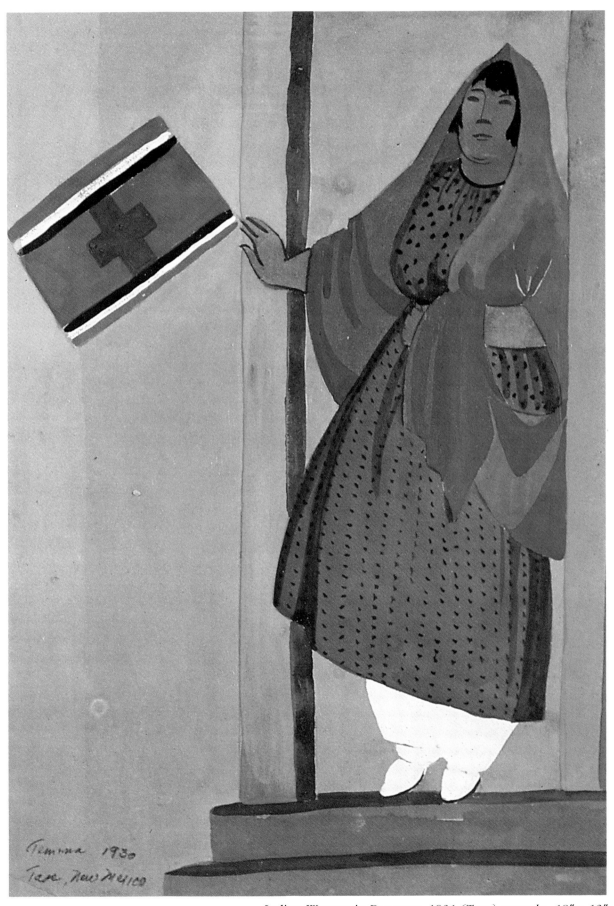

Indian Woman in Doorway, 1931 (Taos), gouache, 18″ × 13″.
Collection of Daniel Gezari

Gloucester Waterfront, 1939 (Gloucester), gouache,
24″ × 18″. Collection of Daniel Gezari

Fishermen, 1939 (Gloucester), gouache, 24″ × 18″.
Collection of Daniel Gezari

Rosie the Lobsterman, *1939 (Gloucester), gouache,*
24" × 18". Collection of Daniel Gezari

Pay Day, 1939 (Gloucester), gouache, 24" × 18".
Collection of Daniel Gezari

Stirring, 1937 (Taxco, Mexico),
charcoal drawing, 24″ × 19″.

Struggle, 1937 (Taxco, Mexico),
charcoal drawing, 24″ × 19″.

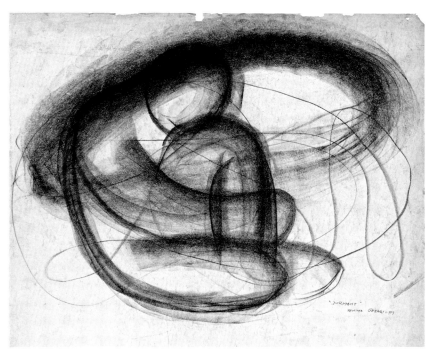

Dormant, 1937 (Taxco, Mexico),
charcoal drawing, 24″ × 19″.

Six Sketches at the Beach, 1938 (Tel Aviv),
pen and ink, 9″ × 12″ and 6″ × 9″.

Murals:

"In modern times, with the expanding of the synagogue from merely a place of worship to a place of assembly for forums, recitals and meetings of all kinds, the attitude toward the decorations on its walls is also undergoing a broadening process. The variety of subject matter at the disposal of the artist is infinite, covering the whole range of human and Jewish aspirations throughout the ages and at the present time. The Jewish artist has a vast field for creative work.

"Murals should occupy a definite place in the architectural layout of a synagogue. At The Society for the Advancement of Judaism, the panels are placed on the south wall, over and flanking the two large entrance doors. Although they have considerable depth, they are painted on a two dimensional plane and do not in any way violate the primary law of mural painting: that, above all, it is a decoration and should take its place on the wall as such. It is the hope of those interested in the development of Jewish creative activities that more efforts will be made in the future to beautify the walls of Jewish places of worship and assembly. There is a definite place for synagogue decoration in our day, just as there was in the days when our forefathers gathered multicolored stones to form mosaic panels that are found in archeological excavations of the elaborately decorated ancient synagogues of the Land of Israel."

(from an article by Temima Gezari in the May 1935 issue of "The Reconstructionist")

Painting the Harvest Mural - 1935.

Restoration of the Mural - 1985.

Harvest Mural, *1935, oils on composition board, 20′ × 8′.*
Synagogue of Cejwin Camp, Port Jervis, New York

In keeping with the philosophy of The Society for the Advancement of Judaism which sees the survival of Judaism only in its creativity and its power to reinterpret and revitalize Jewish tradition, I was called upon to paint a mural for its synagogue in memory of Israel Unterberg, one of the founders of the Society. Having but recently returned from an eight month's visit to Palestine, I chose as my subject "Old and New Elements in Modern Palestine." The approach I used was based on an incident which happened on one of my trips through the Emek. In a field I saw a *halutz* at work, and stopped to speak with him. The sun was mercilessly hot. He rested for a few minutes from his hard work and explained a number of things to me. When I asked him what machinery he used in the field, he held out his hands, palms up. They were rough and calloused; the hands of a worker. "These are my machines," he said, "with them I helped build our colony." My eyes followed the direction of his as they swept with pride across the fields, the huts, the sheds, the barns, and lingered an instant most lovingly as they

Photo by J. Schneider

lit on the new school building just
completed. In it his child was busy
at his studies. His gaze continued its
tour of the surroundings, and then returned to me. "Yes," he repeated,
"these are my machines—and that is
why I am so content." I looked at the
hands. They were the hands of a worker indeed, strong and broad and developed; but the face beaming down upon
these hands was fine and sensitive, despite the many layers of skin, hard-
ened and toughened by sun and wind.
What a wonderful theme to develop in
a painting, I mused: the joy of creat-
ing with one's hands, at once the crud-
est and most developed of all tools. It
conjured up a picture of hands digging
into the soil, hands sowing, hands
weeding, hands gathering in the harvest. Even though machines of steel and
iron break the barren soil of Palestine,
scatter seeds into innumerable fur-
rows, and hasten the ingathering sea-
son by producing tremendous results
in a limited time, the greatest joy comes
to the worker when together with his
companions he tends the flourishing
vegetable plots, picks oranges and
packs grapes. His voice rises in song·

Land of Israel Mural, 1936,
oils on canvas, 4 panels · 30′ × 8′ overall.
Synagogue of the Society for the Advancement of Judiasm,
15 West 86 Street, New York, New York
(Reproduced from "The Reconstructionist," May 1935)

*Study for Land of Israel Mural, 1936,
pencil drawings, two horizontal panels, 20" × 10",
two vertical panels: 16" × 10". Collection of Daniel Gezari*

Woman's Head, 1938 (New York), marble, 8".

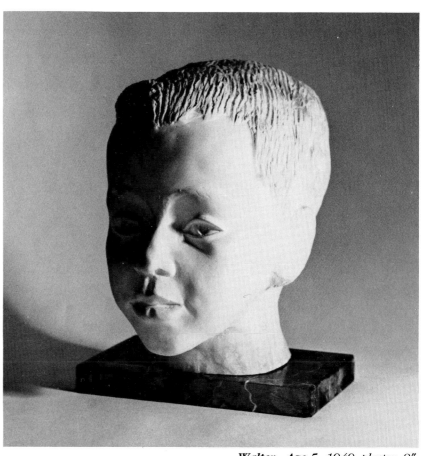

Walter - Age 5, 1949, plaster, 8".

"Im Lo Achshav, Eimatai?" (If not now, when?)
1943 (New York), ceramic plaque, 6″ × 6″.

"Am Matza et ha Moledet, Shav Adam L'adama"
(A nation finds its birthplace, and returns
to the soil.), 1943 (New York), ceramic, 6″.

"Shalom", 1943 (New York), ceramic bowl, 4½″.

African Girl, 1945 (New York),
balsa wood, 12".

Miriam, 1945 (New York),
balsa wood, 18".

Newsboy, 1939 *(New York), painted plaster, 9".*
Collection of Daniel Gezari

photo Dan Gezari

Leaping Lena, 1943 (New York), bronze, 26".
Collection of Daniel Gezari

Father and First Born, Mother and Second Born,
1942, 1944 (New York), terra cotta, 17".

The Stone Cutter, 1946 (New York), bronze, 13".
Collection of Daniel Gezari

Family Circle, *1945 (New York), terra cotta, 15".*

photos Gina Motisi   **Cain and Abel**, *1950, bronze, 60".*

Four Eves, *1949, bronze, 60".*

Daniel - Age 7, 1949, oils on canvas, 16" × 12".
Collection of Daniel Gezari

Traveling to Rocky Point, *1953, mural - oils on transite, 8′ × 4′ (one of two panels).*

Grapes of Wrath, 1950, bronze, 13".
Collection of Daniel Gezari

A Time to Embrace, 1957, oils on canvas, 36″ × 24″.

A Time to Dance, 1957, oils on canvas, 36″ × 24″.

Temima Gezari has organized international exhibits of children's art annually since 1943. "First, the child learns that his work is accepted. We respect and appreciate his effort. With this acceptance he can go on to the exhibition and is proud to see his creation displayed. He looks at other children's work and learns that there are many ways of expressing the same subject. He learns to appreciate the efforts of his peers. Teachers see how other teachers have utilized the art medium to motivate their students. This expands their knowledge, and they go on to the next step in their development.

"Prizes in art are basically destructive and self-defeating. The winner's gratification is gained at the price of the rejection of those who failed. To rule that their best isn't good enough is to inflect needless damage on their self-esteem. I reject the argument that contests provide incentive for productivity.

"Have you ever seen the absorbed concentration of children's faces when they are permitted to do the creative work they love? There is intensity and involvement, no bribe is necessary.

"The young child who learns to please his elders by staying inside the lines of coloring book drawings grows up to be a follower, not a leader. This is the beginning of conformity, the seeds of a mentality that accepts without questioning.

"The creative process gives meaning to life. When we finally learn that we are creative, we have an altogether different feeling about ourselves. When we feel good about ourselves, we feel good about our neighbors. This can lead to a peaceful world, where artists can create for the aesthetic pleasure of all people."

photo Dan Gezari

Morning Song, *1951, bronze, 14".*

Night Prowler, 1951, bronze, 15".

"I have taught many university courses over the years. The first day of class I tell the students that they have all passed the course. There are no examinations at the end of the semester. I am not interested in what dates or names they remember.

"I never teach with a textbook. I tell my students I will give them a list of books to read in their old age, when they are too old to get around to museums and galleries. I want them to have a wonderful experience. Now, while you are young and strong, go out and look and experience. Be humble. Don't say 'You call that art?' Come back again and again. Soon there will be communication, because you have reached out for understanding.

"I have my students work with art materials in all my courses because I believe, as Rousseau said, 'A child may forget what he sees, and sooner still what is said to him, but he will never forget what he has made.'

"I am an artist and an art educator. I love both careers. I don't believe you are really an artist unless you have a concept to share. On the other hand, you are not a good art educator unless you are a functioning artist and have the challenges of the artist before you. An art educator, with skills and capabilities to give the world, is twice blessed."

Temima Gezari · 1952

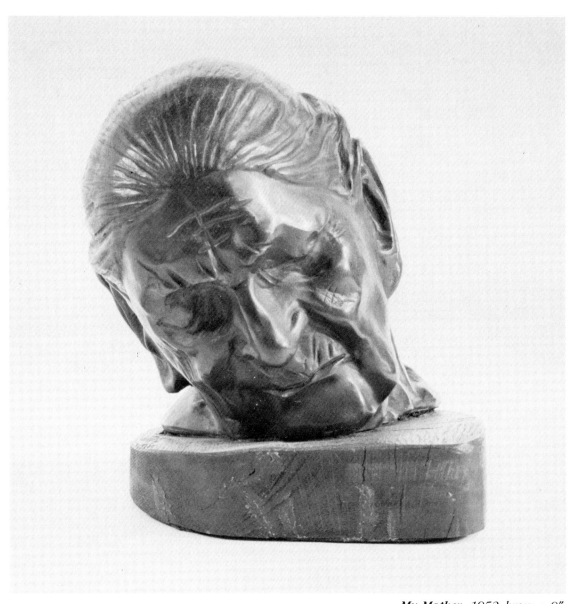

My Mother, 1952, bronze, 9".

63

Beach Stone Series - 1953 to 1966:

King Saul
Growth
Lady in Grey
Town Crier
Two Monks
Cat
Bird in Nest
The Crawler
Sleeping Parakeet
Pink Bird
Leopard with Cubs
Peasant Woman
Filly
Purple Cow
Great Horned Owl
Mare and Foal
A Dickens' Character
Jockey
Friendly Conversation
Monkey
Elephant Boy
The Sun God
Ballerinas
Puppy
Acrobats
Llama
Toreador
Lady with Parasol
Woman with Broom
Goat
Shepherd
Iceskater

Sprinter
Just Born
Lady with Muff
Structure in Red
Gossip
Birth
Wee Lady
Lion
Squirrel
Buddha
Beggar
Circus Clown
Basset Hound
Concave and Convex
Ox
Black Camel
Buddhist Priest
Burning Bush
Little Lamb
New Born
Castilian Dancer
Hassidic Couple
Seated Woman
Pecking Hen
Burning Bush
Sun God
Pharoh
Moses
Rooster and Hen
Horse
No Hands
Had Gadyah
Cow

Dove I
Dove II
Arab Woman
White Lady
Baby Elephant
White Structure
Oriental Boy
Male & Female I
Geisha Girl
Japanese Lady
Mother and Child
Prophet of Peace
Heir Apparent
Indian Corn Dance
Three Generations
Lady in Black
Peacock
Lord High Executioner
Eternal Light
Odalisque
Moment of Silence
Primitive Lady
Rabbi
Dancing Hassid
Hassidic Mother
Bunche Shveig
Boy with Dog
Mother and Infant
Scholar
Prehistoric Family
Wailing Wall
Pharoah

Cat, 1959, beachstone, 8".

Night Riders, 1963, chipped bluestone, 16".

Bathing Beauty, 1959, beachstone, 22".

Stampede, *1963, chipped bluestone, 16".*

Spanish Dancer, 1960, beachstone, 26".

Juggler, 1955, beachstone, 15" high.
Collection of Daniel Gezari

For several years Temima worked with stones and rocks picked up on beaches in their original state, as well as chipped bluestone, cemented together to form figures of people, animals, groups and abstract structures.

"Stooping to pick up a stone, one realizes that lying on the beach they are neutralized by proximity, lost in their numbers. Isolating one stone from the group reveals its uniqueness.

"When I walk on Rocky Point beach, and the children who have been to my studio come running to me with stones they have found and tell me what they have discovered, I am delighted. Everything starts with nature. Add yourself... your imagination, your good mind, your wonderful hands... and you can create something marvelous which has never been known before."

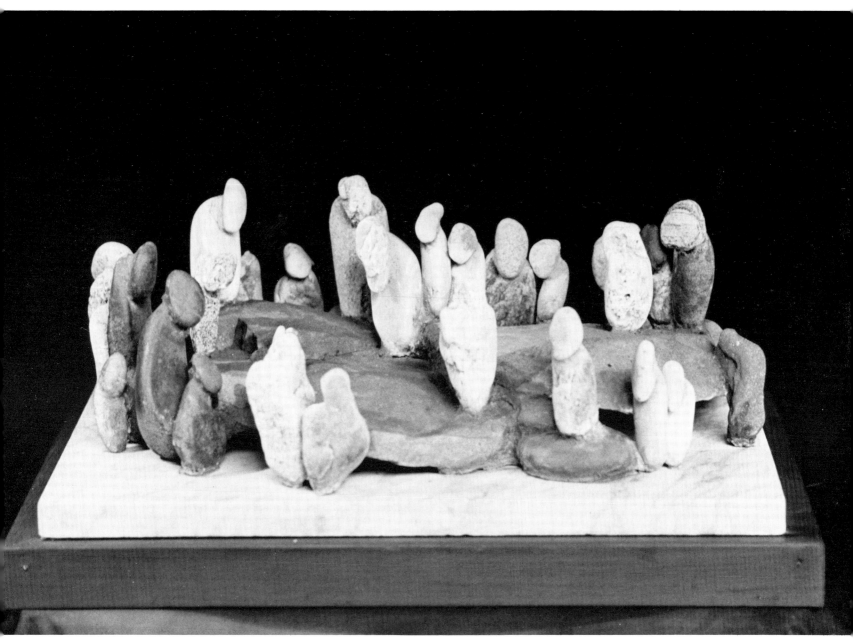

Moment of Silence, 1963, beachstone, 24".

Driftwood Bird, 1964, driftwood, 24".

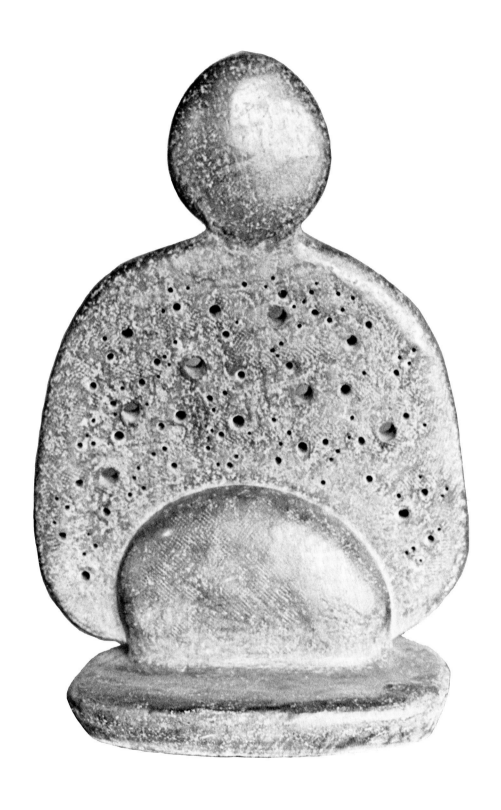

Meditation, 1966, bronze, 26".
Installed at Kibbutz Mishmar Haemek, Israel

The studio at Rocky Point.

Freedom Song, 1965, terra cotta, 18".

At the Wailing Wall, 1966, terra cotta, 18″.

At the Well, 1966, terra cotta, 30" high.
Main Library, Tel Aviv Municipality

Panther, 1966, bronze, 24″.

Moses, 1967, terra cotta stoneware, 30″.
Collection of Mr. and Mrs. Harold Yardlan

Flying Angel, 1967, clay with black patina, 14".

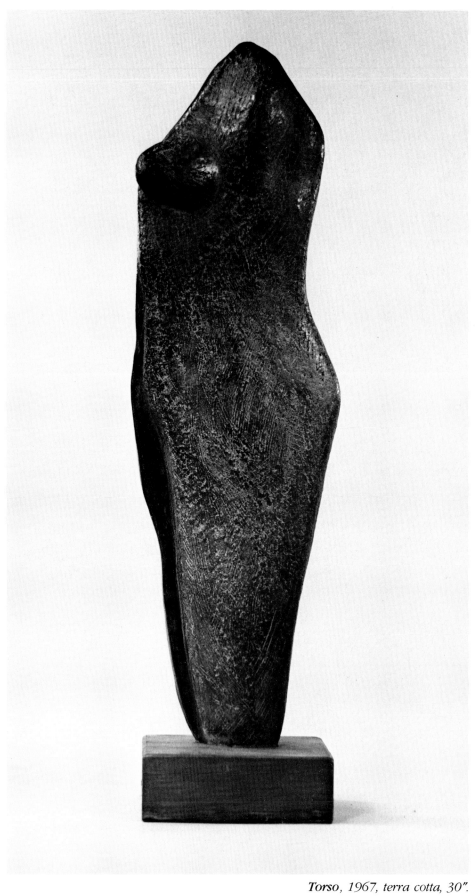

Torso, 1967, terra cotta, 30".

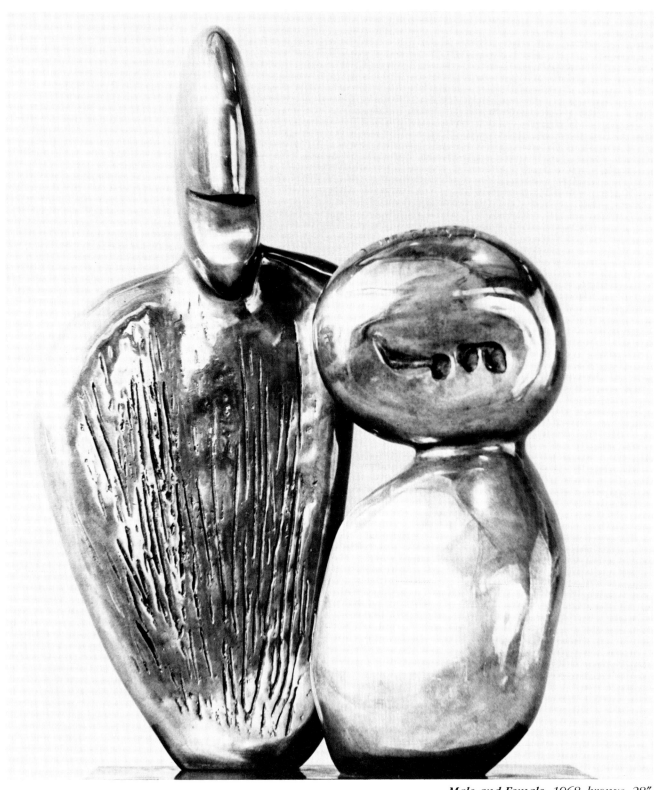

Male and Female, 1968, bronze, 28″.

The Kiss, *1968, bronze, 19".*
Collection of Gena Rowlands and John Cassevetes

The Fruits of War, *1968, clay with*
green patina, 10" × 10".

Black Mother Mourns Her Son, *1964,*
clay with green patina, 12".

Primitive Family, *1968, clay with black patina, 13".*

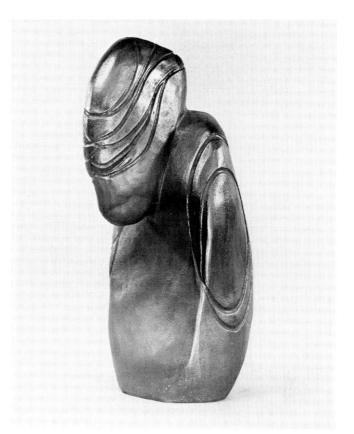

Yizkor, *1968, clay with blue patina, 23".*
Collection of Rabbi and Mrs. Joel Zion

Gossip, *1968, terra cotta with black patina, 22".*

Refugees, *1968, terra cotta with brown patina, 25".*

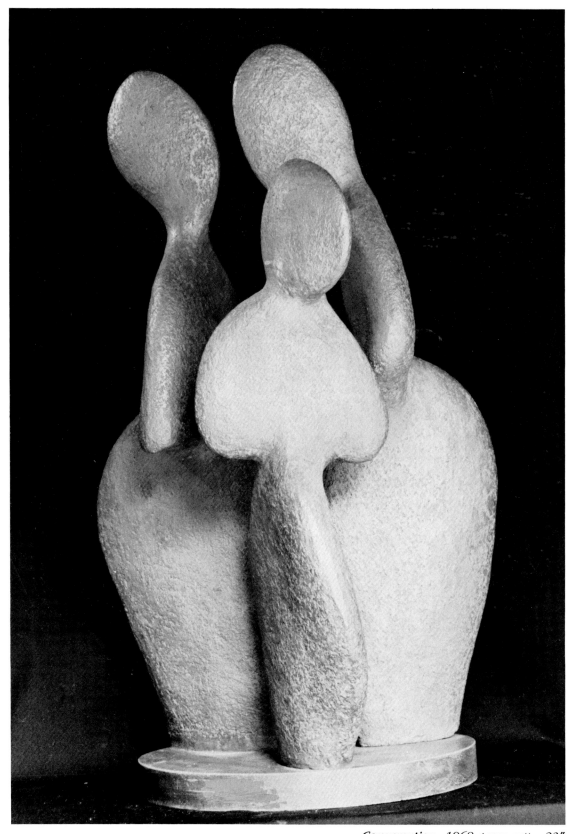

Conversation, 1968, terra cotta, 23".

Job, 1968, bronze, 26".

Prometheus Bound, 1969, terra cotta, 26".

Sails, 1968, terra cotta, 20".

Little Angel, 1969, terra cotta, 19".

Carousel, 1979, terra cotta, 22".

Dancing Hassidim, 1959, terra cotta, 17".

Yeshiva Bachurim (Students), 1968, terra cotta with blue patina, 23".

King Saul, 1967, terra cotta, 33".

Pillar of Salt, 1970, brown clay, 22".

Hassidic Ecstacy, 1970, black clay, 18".

Rebbi and Rebitzen, 1940, glazed ceramic, 6".
Collection of Daniel Gezari

Had Gadya (*Goat*), *1968, bronze, 24".*

Concave and Convex, *1969,*
terra cotta, 17".

Foetus, *1969, terra cotta*
with black patina, 14".

Birth, *1969, terra cotta with*
black patina, 12".

The Golden Calf, 1968, bronze, 24".

Patriarch, 1970, terra cotta, 32".

Totems - 1970:

Love Not War Totem
Judaic Totem
High Holiday Totem
Shabbat Totem
Peace Totem
Black Totem
Generations Totem
Education Totem
Hunger Totem
Conservation Totem
Flag Totem
Column of Peace
Pollution Cycle Totem
Tax Totem
American Indian Totem

"Totems—a form of mass communication—made of brown clay with grog and fired to stoneware. These totems would bear no resemblance to North American Indian totems, except that they would be tall verticals and have various levels. Also, their message had to come across clearly and without difficulty. Therefore, forms had to be simple, realistic, leaving no doubt as to their meaning. Human figures are used throughout, because this entire series is concerned with the needs and struggles of human beings."

Peace Totem, *1970,*
clay, 5' 1".

Conservation Totem, *1970,*
brown clay, 3'.

Generations Totem, *1970,*
brown clay, 4'.

High Holiday Totem, *1970,*
brown clay, 4' 8".

Hunger Totem, *1970,*
brown clay, 4'.

American Indian Totem, *1970,*
brown clay, 5'.

Shabbat Totem, *1970,*
brown clay, 4'.

(bottom tier)

Jewish Contributions to Civilization

a) Abraham - one God,
b) Moses and the Ethical Code,
c) Isaiah - peace and brotherhood,
d) Rabbi Akiba - love of learning

(center tier)

What the World Did to Us:

a) the Roman destruction,
b) the Middle Ages,
c) pogroms in Eastern Europe,
d) the Holocaust.

(upper tier)

The Return to Israel:

Returning to the land and to our
ancient ethical and moral concepts.

Judaic Totem, *1970, cast bronze*
figures in 3 tiers, 5' 10".
Installed at Temple Israel,
Lawrence, New York.

Column of Peace, 1971,
21 clay slabs, 7' 7".

Disc - What's the Good Word?, 1971,
brown clay, 24".

At the beach

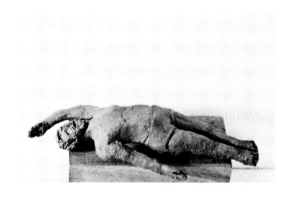

On the Bus

In the Street

Family

Derelicts

Dancers

Singers

Musicians

Sports

At the Beach

Performers

*Working on a children's art exhibit
at the Jewish Museum in New York (1974).*

Africa Series - 1974:

Elmolo Mother and Child
Elmolo Youth
Elmolo Venus
Elmolo Elder
Kukuya Mother
Masai Warrior

Elmolo Mother and Child, *1974, black and
red clay (cast in bronze 1975), 29".*

Kukuya Woman, *1974, black,
brown and red clay, 27".*

Elmolo Youth, *1974, black and red
clay (cast in bronze 1975), 24".*

Masai Warrior, *1974, black,
brown and red clay, 30".*

Small Bronzes - 1975:

Young Girl	Cat
Dancer	Two Rock Dancers
Rabbi at Prayer	Woman Eating Bonbons
Mountain Goat	First Step
Dancers	Margaret Mead
Buddha	Masai Woman
Secretary Bird	Warrior
Dove	Kekuyak Mother
Singer	Baboon
A Couple	Rhino
Pelican	Gazelle
Masai Warrior	Hippo
African Woman	Leopard
Sheep	Zebra
The Rabbi at Prayer	Dikdik
Astronomical Optics Award	Giraffe
Male and Female	Garanuk
Fiddler on the Roof	Topi
Dancing Hassid	Antelope
Wildebeast	Spring Buck
Man in Poncho	Kudo
Flamingo	African Antelope
Baby	Water Buffalo
African Bird	Panther
Pelican	Swan
Baby Elephant	Ostrich
Large Elephant	Crane
Small Elephant	Water Bird
Priestly Blessing	Crested Crane
Old Lady	Bird

Part of the series of about one hundred small bronze figures.

Jungle Roots, *1974, brown clay, 14".*

Anatomy Series - 1976:

Capillaries, black clay, 20″.
Tendons, terra cotta, 20″.
Brain, terra cotta, 21″.
Foetus, terra cotta, 20″.
Cartilege, buff clay, 21″.
Cell, black clay with slip, 17″.
Heart and Lungs, bronze stabile, 17″.
Spinal Section, white clay, 15″.

Nature Series - 1979:

Acacia Tree - Africa, brown clay, 21″.
Bullrushes - Egypt, brown clay, 22″.
Sandpipers - Florida, brown clay, 20″.
Sugar Cane - Cuba, brown clay, 19″.
Jungle Roots - Africa, brown clay, 15″.
Birch Forest - Finland, brown clay, 22″.
Thorns and Thistles - Israel, brown clay, 15″.
Berry Tree - Africa, brown clay, 18″.
Barley in the Wind - Poland, brown clay, 20″.
Cactus - Israel, brown clay, 20″.
Ground Cover - Bermuda, brown clay, 22″.
Fern - Finland, bronze, 28″.
Mussel Shell, bronze, 20″.
Seisel Tree - Africa, brown clay, 17″.
Banyan Tree - Florida, brown clay, 16″.
White Roots - Africa, buff clay, 12″.
Many Moons, white clay, 20″.
Desert Thorn Bush, brown clay, 24″.

The Circle and the Egg Series - 1984:

Cauliflower, buff clay, 22″.
Red Onion, brown clay, 12″.
Winter Squash, brown with buff slip, 10½″.
Green Pepper, brown with buff slip, 19″.
Pineapple, buff clay, 21″.
Tomato, brown with buff slip, 15″.
Red Cabbage, brown clay, 12″.
It's Genetic, brown clay, 14″.

African Plant, 1974, brown clay, 17".

Cell, 1975, black clay with white slip, 18".

Abstraction, 1975, brown clay, 16".

Convolutions, 1975, brown clay, 16".

Sugar Cane - Cuba, 1979, brown clay, 16".

Ground Cover, 1978, brown clay, 16".

Birches - Finland, 1975, brown clay, 18".

Barley - Poland, 1975, brown clay, 17".

Maze, 1974, brown clay, 16".

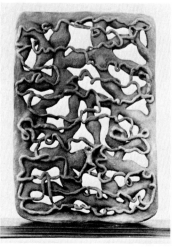

Capillaries, 1975, black clay, 17".

Seisel - Africa, 1974, brown clay, 16".

Berry Vine - Africa, 1974, brown clay, 14".

Fern, 1975, bronze, 29".

Mussel Shell, 1976, bronze, 20".

117

Stabile, 1975, bronze, 17".

Zvi and Temima · 1976

120

Vanessa (Family Series) - 1974:

In Swaddling Clothes
After the Bath
After the Nap
Sitting Up
Crawling
What's in that Hole?
Discovery
Standing Up
Vanessa and Walter
Vanessa and Janet
Vanessa and Temima
Vanessa and Zvi

Suvi (Family Series) - 1977:

The Infant
Pirjo and Suvi
Suvi in Daniel's Hand
The Acrobat
Suvi Dances

Pirjo and Suvi, 1977, bronze, 14".

Janet and Vanessa, 1974, bronze, 16".

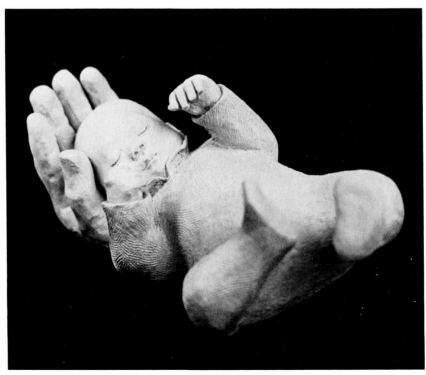

Suvi in Daniel's Hand, 1977, terra cotta, 15".

Vanessa - Newborn, 1974, clay, black patina, 17".

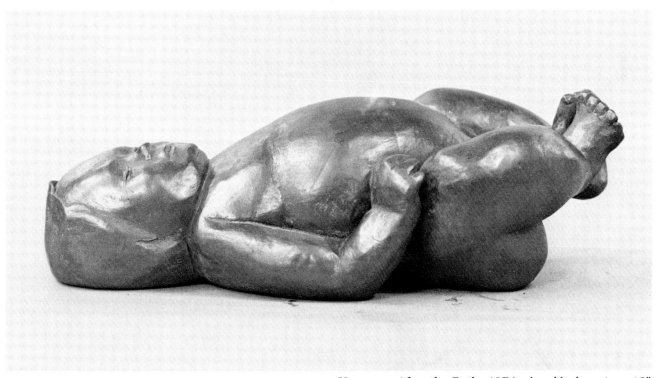

Vanessa - After the Bath, 1974, clay, black patina, 15".

photo S.J. Leicher

"I have always been liberated. At a very early age, I discovered that I was an artist, and had a natural talent to share with the world. That was the key to my personal freedom. However, I think many young female artists today need to be in the feminist movement. I'm all for young women getting together if they don't get fair treatment, having co-op galleries, showing their work and speaking out. I don't blame the women who want their work to be seen; I blame the people who come to exhibitions not to look at paintings, but to see who's going to be there, to see who is and who is not showing. We have put value on the wrong things.

"Years ago I was paid less than a man despite the fact that I was at the top of my field and had brought with me a great deal of experience. Of course, things are much better for me now. But along the way, as a woman, I have had to prove my worth more times than was really necessary. It will have to change, and it will change. I am very optimistic.

"It is important that the female artist never forgets that she also has a most marvelous role to fulfill—that of a mother. My experience with my two children is one I would never give up. Struggling along as an artist while I was raising my children, I learned so much about life. I became a richer artist and a more fulfilled human being. Women can express certain things that men can never reach, because women have the gift of bearing life."

Series of Masks - 1981:
clay with acrylics

My Mother: *She loved flowers openly, and perfume secretly.*

My Father: *He encouraged me in art from the time I was six.*

My Grandmother: *She was a widow, and poor, but had the bearing of a queen.*

My Grandfather: *Frail, and a scholar, his wisdom lit up his face.*

My Great Grandmother: *She was pious, gentle, kind and generous to everyone.*

My Great Grandfather: *He was a wealthy merchant without concern for anyone.*

Zvi's Mother: *Young and beautiful, she suffered in silence, a Holocaust victim.*

Zvi's Father: *A farmer, determined in adversity, true to his faith.*

Zvi's Grandmother: *Kind and gentle, she carried her burden with dignity.*

Zvi's Grandfather: *He was gaunt and stern, enterprising and resourceful.*

Albert Einstein

Harry Truman

Martin Luther King

Eleanor Roosevelt

Golda Meir

Lament, 1978, bronze, 30" high. Collection of the
Yad Vashem Holocaust Museum, Israel.

Students Applaud the Visitors, 1978,
clay and colored slip, 21″.

Worker, 1978, clay and colored slip, 15″.

China Series - 1978:

all in brown clay with slip

Grandfather with Perambulator, 22″.
Man with Rice Bags, 20″.
Market Place, 19″.
Grandmother and Grandson, 19″.
Children's Chorus, 14″.
Father and Daughter, 19″.
Mother and Child, 21″.
Young Girl, 20″.
Going to School, 16″.
Students Applaud the Visitors, 21″.
Worker and Cart, 15″.
Brother and Sister, 16″.
Street Traffic in Peking, 20″.
Riding Home after Work, 18″.
Homeward Bound, 12″.

Sister and Brother, 1978, clay and colored slip, 16".

Mother and Baby, 1978, clay and colored slip, 16".

Israel Series - 1979:

Purim Shpreter *(Clowns), 1979, brown clay with slip, 22".*

Harvest Dance, *1979, brown clay with slip, 20".*

The Sabal (Porter), 1979, brown clay with slip, 18".

Boy with Accordian, 1979, brown clay with slip, 21".

Hassidic Couple, 1979, brown clay with slip, 20".

Grandfather's Blessing, 1979, brown clay with slip, 22". Collection of Mrs. L. Fagnani

Bukharian Man, 1979, brown clay with slip, 20".

Bukharian Women, 1979, brown clay with slip, 20".

Yemenite Bride, 1979, brown clay with slip, 23".

Arab Mother, 1979, brown clay with slip, 22".

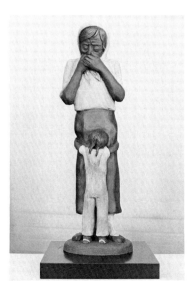

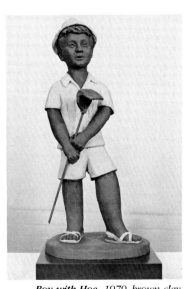

After the Raid, 1979, brown clay with slip, 20". Collection of Mr. and Mrs. A. Molever

Boy with Hoe, 1979, brown clay with slip, 21".

Kibbutz Mother, 1979, brown clay with slip, 22".

Kibbutz Father, 1979, brown clay with slip, 22".

American Eagle - Crucifixion, 1971, brown and buff clay with white slip, mounted on wood, 36".

Going to School - China, 1978, clay and colored slip, 15".
Collection of Daniel Gezari

photo S.J. Leicher

Temima Gezari has taken line drawings done by her granddaughter Suvi, when she was two years old, and created a series of sculptures to show "that children instinctively have the knowledge of our world. It amazes me, what a child can do with one stroke."

"What I have done is to demonstrate my philosophy of art, that the fundamental principles of art can be found in the world of a two-year old...work which the child does instinctively.

"The art medium provides children with a universal language, through which they can express ideas and feelings that they may find difficult to convey in words. Through manipulation of basic materials, children develop confidence, courage, and a creative spirit. People, especially parents, must be brought to the realization that art should become part of everyone's experience to develop to their greatest capability.

"A child's creativity and perception of the world must be encouraged. An adult may look at a child's painting and say, 'I never saw a purple cow,' when the child proudly holds it up. Of course, the child hasn't either, but was looking with imagination. An understanding parent or teacher will tell the child, "That's the most beautiful cow I've ever seen!"

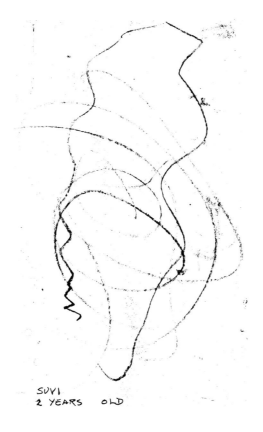

SUVI
2 YEARS OLD

Abstraction #1, 1979, black clay.

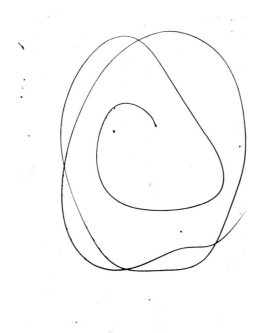

SUVI - 2 YEARS OLD

Abstraction #2, 1979, brown clay.

135

New Atlas, 1955, bronze, 29".
Collection of Daniel Gezari

Little David, 1982, buff clay with acrylics, 20".
(Childhood Fantasies Series)
Collection of Ira and Elaine Yanowitz

Childhood Fantasy Series - 1982:
clay with acrylics

The Body Builder (Marc Atkins), 20″.
The Pirate (Vanessa Gezari), 25″.
An Acting Person (Amanda Reiss), 20″.
Ice Cream Lady (Lee Sheloush), 20″.
Little David (David Yanowitz), 20″.
Ballerina (Suvi Gezari), 21″.
Leader of the Parade (Sam Gezari), 25″.
I'm a Lady (Vanessa Gezari), 26″.
See My Hat! (Suvi Gezari), 25″.
Riding a Dinosaur (Matthew Stine), 24″.
Speed Car Driver (Benjamin Ritt), 21″.

Animal Series - 1983:

Hippo, brown clay, 18″.
Ostrich, brown and buff clay, 24″.
Bear, brown clay, 16″.
Cheetah, ochre patina, 24″.
Antelope, brown clay, 18″.
Gazelle, white clay, 23″.
Baboon, brown clay, 26″.
Great Horned Owl, terra cotta, 22″.
Cat, terra cotta, 22″.

photo Elena Evitta

Woman of Valor, *1985,*
bone clay, 22".

Suffragettes, *1985,*
bone clay, 22".

Union Label, *1985,*
bone clay, 17".

N.O.W., *1985,*
red clay, 22".

Sarah, *1985,*
red clay 19".

The Breeder, *1985,*
bone clay, 21".

Bag Lady, *1985,*
bone clay, 21".

Sex Symbol, *1985,*
bone clay, 22".

Rachel, *1985,*
red clay, 20".

Rebecca, *1985,*
red clay, 19".

Ruth and Naomi, *1985,*
red clay, 18".

Deborah the Judge, *1985,*
terra cotta, 17".

"For the artist, the discipline of the craft must always be maintained, that is, the understanding of space, color and form. You, the artist, must be dedicated to the task you have set for yourself. Despite its heavy and relentless demands, it is a task from which you would never wish to be free.

"I am not a competitive artist. I am not interested in being better than anybody else. The person I compete with is myself. I am happy when people like my work, but if I am not satisfied, their compliments will have no meaning for me. It is impossible to be a free, creative human being if you try to satisfy someone else's standard of what is good. I have always set my own standards and gone my own merry way.

"I am not an artist who says 'let people get what they can out of my art.' I want the world to see my work, to understand and love it. When I put something down in stone or clay, I am sharing my insights into nature, my feelings about humanity.

"My art reflects my fundamental concerns and values. My sculpture represents the integration of traditional ideas of social justice, moral and ethical concepts with a personal interpretation of their application to contemporary life in our world today.

"I love the human figure, its organic design and engineering perfection. The part reflects the whole; in the leaf we see the tree, in the cell the future is born.

"I believe that human beings are essentially creators. There is no limit to their potential, or to the heights they can reach, if they align themselves with the creative energy in the universe."

Temima Gezari - 1985.

Woman Series - 1985

Biblical Women - 1985

Catalog of Works:

PENCIL DRAWINGS (Partial List):

Egyptian Mother, 1934, 24″ × 18″.

Three Generations, 1934, 30″ × 24″.

Hassidic Newlyweds, 1934, 30″ × 24″.

Three Arab Women

Az Der Rebbi Tantzt, Tantzen alle Hassidim,
   1934, 18″ × 24″.

The Sage, 1934, 18″ × 12″.

Jericho, 1934, 18″ × 12″.

Donkey Ballet, 1934, 18″ × 24″.

Arabs at Rest, 1934, 24″ × 18″.

Arab Mother, 1934, 24″ × 18″.

Stone Cutter, 1934, 24″ × 18″.

My Grandfather, 1932, 15″ × 12″.

The House of My Teacher, Emil Bisttram,
   1931, 9″ × 11½″.

Jonah and the Whale, 1929, 12½″ × 9½″.

My Studio (Taos), 1931, 9″ × 11½″.

Taos Pueblo, 1931, 11″ × 15″.

Landscape in Triangles, 1932, 10″ × 14″.

Vertical and Horizontal #1, 1932, 10″ × 14″.

Vertical and Horizontal #2, 1932, 10″ × 10″.

Satat (Arab Stone Cutter), 1934, 10″ × 20″.

Hamagish (The Helper), 1934, 24″ × 18″.

The Old City of Jerusalem, 1934, 20″ × 14″.

Big Business - Cigarette Vendor, 1938, 17″ × 23″.

Big Business - Shoe Repair Man, 1938, 17″ × 23″.

Big Business - Sabal (Porter), 1938, 17″ × 24″.

Donkeys, 1934, 24″ × 18″.

Study of a Head, 1927, 15″ × 13″.

Standing Figure, 1927, 18″ × 12″.

Reclining Figure, 1927, 18″ × 12″.

Seated Nude, 1925, 18″ × 12″.

Four Sisters, 1932, 19″ × 12″.

Rocks - Monbegan Island, 1939, 15″ × 14″.

Tree of Life (Circle in a Square), 1930, 15″ × 13″.

Tree Study, 1932, 21″ × 15″.

Figure, 1925, 18″ × 12″.

Figure, 1926, 18″ × 12″.

Emil Bisttram's House, 1931, 11″ × 9″.

Indian Woman, 1931, 15″ × 13″.

CHALK DRAWINGS (Partial List):

Standing Nude, 1927, 18″ × 12″.

Torso, 1927, 18″ × 12″.

Head, 1927, 18″ × .12″.

CHARCOAL DRAWINGS (Partial List):

Dormant, 1937, 24″ × 19″.

Struggle, 1937, 24″ × 19″.

Stirring, 1937, 24″ × 19″.

OIL PAINTINGS (Partial List):

Abstract Landscape, 1932 (Taos), oils on canvas.

Daniel - Age 7, 1949, oil on canvas, 16″ × 12″.

Traveling to Rocky Point, 1953, oils on transit, 8′ × 4′.

A Time to Embrace, 1957, oils on canvas, 36″ × 24″.

A Time to Dance, 1957, oils on canvas, 36″ × 24″.

GOUACHES (Partial List):

Taos, New Mexico 1951.

Indian Woman in Doorway, 18″ × 13″.

Taos Indian Man, 1930, 19″ × 13″.

Indian Woman, 1930, 14″ × 10″.

Gloucester, 1939.

On the Dock, 24″ × 18″.

Rosie the Lobsterman, 24″ × 18″.

Fishermen, 24″ × 18″.

Pay Day, 24″ × 18″.

Sailboats, 20″ × 16″.

Gloucester Waterfront, 24″ × 18″.

Waterfront Shacks, 24″ × 18″.

Fishing Boats, 24″ × 18″.

LITHOGRAPHS (Partial List):

Fish for Shabbat, 1935, 15″ × 10″.

The World Situation (Lower East Side), 1935, 19″ × 15″.

The Little Presser, 1935, 18″ × 13″.

Under the Bridge, 1935, 14″ × 11″.

Shabbos Shpatzir, 1934, 19″ × 13″.

Wash Day - Kibbutz, 1938, 15″ × 11″.

STONE AND WOOD SCULPTURE:

Miriam, 1943, painted balsa wood.

African Girl, 1943, painted balsa wood, 12″.

Old Woman, 1943, painted balsa wood, 12″.

Woman with Jug, 1943, painted balsa wood.

Father and Daughter, 1949, balsa wood, 39″.

Male Head, 1961, soapstone, 14″.

Mother and Child, 1961, soapstone, 14″.

Marble Head, 1943, marble, 6″.

Fieldstone Head, 1949, fieldstone, 15″.

First Grandchild, 1961, soapstone, 9″.

Curious Goose, 1959, pebble mosaic sculpture, 33″.

Rooster, 1959, ceramic mosaic sculpture, 30″.

TIME SERIES - 1957:

Oils on canvas, 36″ × 24″.

A Time to Be Born

A Time to Die

A Time to Mourn

A Time to Dance

A Time to Plant

A Time to Build

A Time to Embrace

CLAY SCULPTURE:

Moses, 1967, high fired clay, 32″.

Moses, 1970, brown clay.

Blowing with the Wind, brown clay, 19″.

Yizkor, 1966, terra cotta, 20″.

Tiyul Shabbat, 1962, terra cotta, 14″.

White Dove, 1968, terra cotta, 18″.

War Widow, 1969, brown clay, 12″.

Maiden, 1956, terra cotta, 18″.

Seated Woman, 1953, terra cotta, 14″.

Abstract Mother and Child, 1968, terra cotta, 13″.

Paternal Blessing, 1958, terra cotta, 12″.

Trinidad George, 1967, brown clay, 14″.

Barbados Jane, 1967, brown clay, 15″.

Fifth Avenue Lady, 1967, brown clay, 15″.

Freedom Song, 1965, terra cotta, 18″.

Rebbi, 1968 terra cotta, 20″.

Three Generations, 1968, terra cotta, 30″.

White Lady, 1968, terra cotta, 4″.

Concave & Convex, 1968, terra cotta, 17″.

Birth, 1969, terra cotta, 12″.

Conversation, 1968, terra cotta, 20″.

Gossip, 1969, terra cotta, 12″.

*American Eagle - Crucifixion,*1971,
  clay on wood, 36″.

What's the Good Word?, 1970, brown clay, 22″.

Tower of Babel, 1970, brown clay, 28″.

Boys with Guitar, 1963, terra cotta, 11″.

Sam with Ball, 1981, terra cotta, 12″.

Man's Head, 1954, soapstone, 14″.

Marble Head, 1943, 6″.

Fieldstone Head, 1949, fieldstone, 15″.

Rabbi and Rebbitzen, 1940, glazed ceramic, 6″.

Abstract Mother and Child, 1968, terra cotta, 16″.

Eternal Light, 1968, terra cotta, 34″.

Night Riders, 1968, terra cotta, 28″.

Three Generations, 1968, terra cotta, 29″.

The Scholar, 1968, terra cotta, 21″.

Harlequin, 1968, terra cotta, 34″.

Ram, 1968, terra cotta, 27″.

Baboon, 1968, terra cotta, 26″.

Dove, 1968, terra cotta, 16″.

Chess Family, 1968, terra cotta, 33″.

Oriental Mother, 1968, terra cotta, 21″.

Mare and Foal, 1968, terra cotta, 24″.

Maiden, 1968, terra cotta, 31″.

Growth, 1968, terra cotta, 24″.

Zvi and Einstein, 1968, terra cotta, 15″.

Bird, 1968, terra cotta, 12″.

Primitive Family, 1968, terra cotta, 13″.

"Time for Tea", 1968, terra cotta, 12″.

LARGE BRONZES:

Stone Cutter, 1946, 13″.

Leaping Lena, 1943, 26″.

Lament, 1978, 30″.

Meditation, 1966, 26″.

New Atlas, 1968, 29″.

My Mother, 1970, 9″.

Elmolo Youth, 1975, 24″.

Elmolo Mother and Child, 1975, 29″.

Winged Victory, 1972, 27″.

The Kiss, 1970, 19″.

Pirjo and Suvi, 1977, 14″.

Janet and Vanessa, 1974, 16″.

Male and Female, 1968, 28″.

Had Gadya (Goat), 1974, 24″.

The Golden Calf, 1970, 24″.

Panther, 1974, 24″.

Job, 1968, 26″.

Morning Song, 1951, 14″.

Night Prowler, 1951, 15″.

The Four Eves, 1949, 60″.

Cain and Abel, 1950, 5′.

TOTEMS - 1970:

Brown clay.

Love Not War Totem

Judaic Totem

High Holiday Totem

Shabbat Totem

Peace Totem

Black Totem

Generations Totem

Education Totem

Hunger Totem

Conversation Totem

Flag Totem

Column of Peace

Pollution Cycle Totem

Tax Totem

American Indian Totem

BOOKS:

Footprints and New Worlds (1957),
  Reconstructionist Press, New York (Fourth
  edition, Board of Jewish Education, New York).

The Jewish Kindergarten (1944), Union of
  American Hebrew Congregations, New York
  (Co-authored with Deborah Pessin).

Gateway to Jewish Song (1934), Behrman
  Book House, New York (Illustrator).

Children of the Emek (1937), Furrow Press,
  New York (Illustrator).

Hillel's Happy Holidays (1939), Union of
  American Hebrew Congregation, Cincinnati
  (Illustrator).

BEACH STONE SERIES - 1950 to 1966:

King Saul
Growth
Lady in Grey
Town Crier
Two Monks
Cat
Bird in Nest
The Crawler
Sleeping Parakeet
Pink Bird
Leopard with Cubs
Peasant Woman
Filly
Purple Cow
Great Horned Owl
Mare and Foal
A Dickens' Character
Jockey
Friendly Conversation
Monkey
Elephant Boy
Ballerinas
Puppy
Acrobats
Llama
Toreador
Lady with Parasol
Woman with Broom
Goat
Shepherd
Iceskater

Dove I
Dove II
Arab Woman
White Lady
Baby Elephant
White Structure
Oriental Boy
Male & Female I
Geisha Girl
Japanese Lady
Mother and Child
Prophet of Peace
Heir Apparent
Indian Corn Dance
Three Generations
Lady in Black
Peacock
Lord High Executioner
Eternal Light
Odalisque
Moment of Silence
Primitive Lady
Rabbi
Dancing Hassid
Hassidic Mother
Bunche Shveig
Boy with Dog
Mother and Infant
Scholar
Prehistoric Family
Wailing Wall
Pharoah

Sprinter
Just Born
Lady with Muff
Structure in Red
Gossip
Birth
Wee Lady
Lion
Squirrel
Buddha
Beggar
Circus Clown
Basset Hound
Concave and Convex
Dancer
Black Camel
Buddhist Priest
Little Lamb
New Born
Castilian Dancer
Hassidic Couple
Seated Woman
Pecking Hen
Burning Bush
Sun God
Pharaoh
Moses
Rooster and Hen
Horse
No Hands
Had Gadyah
Cow

CHIPPED BLUESTONE SCULPTURE - 1963:

Camel, 10".
Fencers, 10".
Ritual Dance, 10".
Lion, 8".
Don Quixote #1, 11".
Don Quixote #2, 24".
Family, 11".
Anniversary Dance, 10".
Elephant, 7".
Stampede, 14".
Night Riders, 16".
Abstract Cluster, 12".
Two Clowns, 12".
Seated Man, 10".

LARGE BEACH STONE SCULPTURE:

Moment of Silence
Academic Procession, 21".
Bride and Groom, 12".
Prophet of Peace, 33".
Oriental Lady, 20".
The Juggler, 18".
Indian Dancer, 29".
Fantasy Bird, 17".
Sleeping Dog, 7".
Pecking Chick, 9".

Pecking Hen, 16".
Sitting Hen, 16".
Had Gadya, 16".
Hassidic Couple, 15".
Resting Cow, 11".
Llama, 11".
Burning Bush
Sitting Horse, 15".
Pharaoh, 10".
The Sacrifice, 15".
Ox, 10".

SMALL BRONZES - 1975:

Young Girl
Dancer
Rabbi at Prayer
Mountain Goat
Dancers
Buddha
Secretary Bird
Dove
Singer
A Couple
Pelican
Masai Warrior
African Woman
Sheep
The Rabbi at Prayer
Astronomical Award
Male and Female
Fiddler on the Roof
Dancing Hassid
Wildebeast
Man in Poncho
Flamingo
Baby

African Bird
Pelican
Baby Elephant
Dancer
At Prayer
Goat
Fox
Japanese Lady
Rooster
Horse
Opera Singer
Owl
Little Angel
Sleeping Child
Large Elephant
Small Elephant
Priestly Blessing
Old Lady
Cat
Two Rock Dancers
Woman Eating Bonbons
First Step
Margaret Mead
Masai Woman

Warrior
Kekuyak Mother
Baboon
Rhino
Gazelle
Hippo
Leopard
Zebra
Dikdik
Giraffe
Garanuk
Topi
Antelope
Spring Buck
Kudo
African Antelope
Water Buffalo
Panther
Swan
Ostrich
Crane
Water Bird
Crested Crane

BEHOLD THE PEOPLE - 1972:

Singers
Dancers
Musicians
Actors
Sports
At the Beach
In the Street
On the Bus
Senior Citizens
The Derelicts
At the Circus

VANESSA (Family Series) - 1974:

In Swaddling Clothes
After the Bath
After the Nap
Sitting Up
Crawling
What's in that Hole?
Discovery
Standing Up
Vanessa and Walter
Vanessa and Janet
Vanessa and Temima
Vanessa and Zvi

AFRICA SERIES - 1974:

Elmolo Mother, bronze, 29″.
Elmolo Youth, bronze, 24″.
Elmolo Venus, black and red clay, 27″.
Elmolo Mother, black and red clay, 27″.
Elmolo Elder, black, red and brown clay, 15½″.
Elmolo Youth, black and red clay, 24″.
Kukuya Mother, black, brown, red clay, 27″.
Masai Warrior, black, brown, red clay, 30″.

ANATOMY SERIES - 1976:

Capillaries, black clay, 20″.
Tendons, terra cotta, 20″.
Brain, terra cotta, 21″.
Foetus, terra cotta, 20″.
Cartilage, buff clay, 21″.
Cell, black clay with slip, 17″.
Heart and Lungs, bronze and stabile, 17″.
Spinal Section, white clay, 15″.

SUVI (Family Series) - 1977:

The Infant
Pirjo and Suvi
Suvi in Daniel's Hand
The Acrobat
Suvi Dances

CHINA SERIES - 1978:

All in brown clay with slip.
Grandfather with Perambulator, 22″
Man with Rice Bags, 20″.
Market Place, 19″.
Grandmother and Grandson, 19″.
Children's Chorus, 14″.
Father and Daughter, 19″.
Mother and Child, 21″.
Young Girl, 20″.
Going to School, 16″.
Students Applaud the Visitors, 21″.
Worker and Cart, 15″.
Brother and Sister, 16″.
Street Traffic in Peking, 20″.
Riding Home After Work, 18″.
Homeward Bound, 12″.

SOUTH AMERICAN SERIES - 1978:
Columbian Mother, brown clay, 25".
Man on a Bicycle, 17".
Man on Burro, 17".
Old Woman, 16".
Pregnant Woman, 26".
Woman with Bag of Sticks, 19".
Man, 25".

ISRAEL SERIES - 1979:
Brown clay with slip.
After the Raid, 20".
Grandfather's Blessing, 22".
Kibbutz Mother, 22".
Kibbutz Father, 22".
Hassidic Couple, 20".
Yemenite Bride, 23".
Boy with Hoe, 21".
Harvest Dance, 20".
Arab Mother, 22".
The Sabal (Porter), 18".
Arab on Donkey, 20".
Boy with Accordian, 21".
Purim Shpreter, 22".
Bukbarian Woman, 20".
Bukbarian Man, 20".

SERIES OF MASKS - 1981:
Buff clay with acrylics.
My Mother
My Father
My Grandmother
My Grandfather
My Great Grandmother
My Great Grandfather
Zvi's Mother
Zvi's Father
Zvi's Grandmother
Zvi's Grandfather
Albert Einstein
Golda Meir
Eleanor Roosevelt
Martin Luther King
President Truman

CHILDHOOD FANTASY
SERIES - 1982:
Buff clay with acrylics.
The Body Builder, Marc Atkins, 20".
The Pirate, Vanessa Gezari, 25".
An Acting Person, Amanda Reiss, 20".
Ice Cream Lady, Lee Sheloush, 20".
Little David, David Yanowitz, 20".
Ballerina, Suvi Gezari, 21".
Leader of the Parade, Sam Gezari, 25".
I'm a Lady, Vanessa Gezari, 26".
See My Hat!, Suvi Gezari, 25".
Riding a Dinosaur, Matthew Stine, 24".
Speed Car Driver, Benjamin Ritt,, 21".

ANIMAL SERIES - 1983:
Hippo, brown clay, 18".
Ostrich, brown and buff clay, 24".
Bear, brown clay, 16".
Cheetah, ochre patina, 24".
Antelope, brown clay, 18".
Gazelle, white clay, 23".
Baboon, brown clay, 26".
Great Horned Owl, terra cotta, 22".
Cat, terra cotta, 22".

THE CIRCLE AND EGG SERIES - 1984:
Cauliflower, buff clay, 22".
Red Onion, brown clay, 12".
Winter Squash, brown with buff slip, 10½".
Green Pepper, brown with buff slip, 19".
Pineapple, buff clay, 21".
Tomato, brown with buff slip, 15".
Red Cabbage, brown clay, 12".
It's Genetic, brown clay, 14".

FILMSTRIPS:
Growing Through Art (1955).
Art and the Growing Child (1956 winner
    of the Silver Reel Award of the Film Council
    of America and the 1957 Scholastic Award).
Miniature Stone Sculpture (1963).
The Art of Israeli Children (1963).
The Patriarchs (1977).

WOMAN SERIES - 1985:
Buff clay.
The Breeder, 21".
Woman of Valor, 21".
Suffragettes, 22".
Bag Lady, 21".
Sex Symbol, 21".
The Union Label, 17".
National Organization for Women, 22".

BIBLICAL WOMEN - 1985:
Terra cotta.
Sarah, 19".
Rebeccah, 19".
Rachel, 20".
Ruth and Naomi, 18".
Deborah the Judge, 17".

NATURE SERIES:
Acacia Trees - Africa, brown clay, 21".
Bullrushes - Egypt, brown clay, 22".
Sandpipers - Florida, brown clay, 20".
Sugar Cane - Cuba, brown clay, 19".
Jungle Roots - Africa, brown clay, 15".
Birch Forest - Finland, brown clay, 22".
Thorns and Thistles - Israel, brown clay, 15".
Berry Tree - Africa, brown clay, 18".
Barley - Poland, brown clay, 20".
Cactus - Israel, brown clay, 20".
Ground Cover - Bermuda, brown clay, 22".
Fern - Finland, bronze, 28".
Mussel Shell, bronze, 20".
Seisel Tree - Africa, brown clay, 17".
Banyan Tree - Florida, brown clay, 16".
White Roots - Africa, buff clay, 12".
Many Moons, white clay, 20".
Desert Thorn Bush, brown clay, 24"
Driftwood #1, brown clay, 22".
Driftwood #2, brown clay, 20".
Driftwood #3, brown clay, 21".
Driftwood Totem, buff clay, 40".
Many Moons, buff clay, 20".